Holiday Wisdom

Open your eyes to your Yule Tide Ride

in New Year Cheer

Robert Wilson

Editing by Amy Lignor

DEDICATION

This book is dedicated to my Brothers and Sisters: Jack Wilson, Randy Wilson, Kathy Roti, and Mary Engel

Holiday Wisdom
By Robert A. Wilson

For more books like this one, visit Robert A. Wilson's website at:
http://cowboy-wisdom.com/

Printed in the United States of America
The publisher offers discounts on this book when ordered in bulk quantities. For more information, contact Sales Department, Phone 815-290-9605, Email:
sales@FreedomOfSpeechPublishing.com

Freedom of Speech Publishing, Leawood KS, 66224
www.FreedomOfSpeechPublishing.com
ISBN: 1938634225
ISBN-13: 978-1-938634-22-2

A SPECIAL THANK YOU TO YOU!

On behalf of everyone at Freedom Of Speech Publishing, thank you for choosing Holiday Wisdom for your reading enjoyment.

As an added bonus and special thank you, for purchasing Holiday Wisdom, you can enjoy discounts and special promotions on other Freedom of Speech Publishing products. Visit www.freedomeofspeech.com/vip to learn more.

We are committed to providing you with the highest level of customer satisfaction possible. If for any reason you have questions or comments, we are delighted to hear from you. Email us at cs@freedomofspeechpublishing.com or visit our website at: http://freedomofspeechpublishing.com/contact-us-2/.

If you enjoyed Holiday Wisdom, visit www.freedomofspeechpublishing.com for a list of similar books or upcoming books.

Again, thank you for your patronage. We look forward to providing you more entertainment in the future.

Contents

Acknowledgements

A huge thank you goes out to my Mom and Dad who have passed for being my parents, and the work ethic and moral values they instilled in me. I understand I wasn't always the easiest child…

I thank my family and extended family: Nieces, Nephews, Aunts, Uncles, Cousins, Sisters and Brothers for being a part of my life.

I thank every one of my friends for being part of my life.

I thank Amy Lignor (www.thewritecompanion.com): published author, editor, ghostwriter, reviewer - who writes dynamic articles to expand your brand and enhance your bottom line.

I thank God, Mrs. Universe, the womb of

unconditional love and enterprising energies, all people, spiritual ethers, metaphysical realms, physical playgrounds, mystical magical heavens of miracles, and all realized and unrealized sources in the cosmos, for opening the way to authorize and allow me to experience my life, *my way.*

I thank all my listeners and guests on *Cowboy Wisdom NLI Radio* at www.blogtalkradio.com/cwbywsdm.

I thank everybody who buys and reads to expand their life in a perfect way

I am thankful for my life everyday in every way under grace in a perfect way.

I love life and life loves me!

Author's Note

Thank you for purchasing *Holiday Wisdom*

Open your eyes to your Yule Tide Ride in New Year Cheer

May you experience a Happy Thanksgiving energizing your Merry Christmas electrifying your Prosperous New Year opening out a Happy Easter galvanizing your Cinco De Mayo glorifying your Joyous Memorial Day exhilarating your Happy Fourth of July enlivening your liberating Labor Day and exalting your Happy Halloween!!!

Happy Holidays to you and your family. May your Holiday Wisdom flow in lavish luxury instantly to eternity!!!

May life always and in all ways flow in
lavish avalanches of affluent abundances
now to eternity in the right way, in a
loving way, under grace in a divine
blessed way, and in divine order...**NOW**!

With a Smile in My Heart

Robert A. Wilson

Preface

Happy Holidays to one and all!!! Unmask your Holiday Cheer with Cowboy Wisdom Innovation Coaching Holiday Wisdom to whimsically initiate Santa Claus daringness optimizing magnificence within you mesmerizing your family holidays with your magnanimous essence. As your Holiday Spirit Soars your eyes open to see you are the gift to your family and world.

As your read Holiday Wisdom open your inner landscape to realize that Holiday Wisdom is written in first person for your highest emotional expansion. So now say "I choose to read out-loud for maximum outcome to energize my Holiday Spirit turning on my internal glowing Christmas Lights allowing the world to see me beam esteemed free flowing love to my family and all the people of the world."

As my Thanksgiving Thankfulness opens my Christmas Eyes emancipates my New Year's ears to hear my Easter Awakening freeing my Memorial Day daredevil unleashing my Fourth of July Independence unmasks my Labor Day Grittiness highlighting my Halloween Hallowedness. I show the world I am the holiday hierophant seeing the world as free flowing love with people unveiling their goodwill towards each other in a serene sensational way under grace in a divine blessed way and in divine order now.

Wampanoag Wisdom and Pilgrim Pluck say Happy Thanksgiving

Wampanoag Wisdom & Pilgrim Pluck say "Happy Thanksgiving" today to all the people in the United States, in a joyous way, allowing people to unite in a bright light of love and gratitude.

Because they choose to let go of their differences in order to 'break bread'; threading new understandings in the universal landscape by opening a clear blue sky filled with beautification highlighting communication.

Opens the way for their oracle orators to pave a pathway of peace and prosperity, bequeathing to the United States and world populace today...

A poetic prophesy to enjoy this Thanksgiving holiday is their divine right in the right way...in a loving way, under grace, in a picture perfect way.

By harmonizing optimum love, idyllically declaring ardent 'YEA'-sayer cheer blesses my Thanksgiving Festivities for all to share in a shiny new way.

Unsealing my daring ingenuity, sanctions me by displaying my rays of sun from affluent accomplishments this year. So now I take a bow for my rabble rousing will…

Lighting up my inner resolve to say I was challenged! I was challenged to solve by being involved, divulging the fact that I am in willing to open my eyes to see the light of wisdom in all my challenges.

I now live inside my inner wise in a rich regal way.

When I am listening to my core clairvoyants televise my opulent outcomes, brightly beaming the beautifications of my clever communication and enticing my drum roll listening, unsheathes…

My proficiency and correlates the broadcasting with firsthand keenness - with all solar orators canonizing our commodore omniscience…

Accenting our appreciation, the uniqueness of our clever, differing visions that expand the winning acumen in people's hearts to experience life in a new way…freeing mature innovation.

Because I detached from the attachment of 'I am right, the world is wrong' was a blight of bigotry that bit my signatory butt that mirrored the fear of dictators…

Licking their wounds bound in time, binding
their minds, blinding their visions with the
incisions of their decisions…

With their 'big-go' egos, seeking respect from
people and the world because they subliminally
suspect…

They disrespect themselves because they could
smell their inner hell pell-mell-ling… The
smell from their commode when they dropped a
lode, peevishly snuck into their bureaucrat
nostrils giving them a hint that the crap they
were rapping did 'stink of the fink of the over
think'…

Unties the lies, putting the fly in there
disappoint when they hear bureaucrats put forth
a masculine fallacy that they are tough and in
control, but in reality…

That doused them with mouse-'ism' revealing to
them they are doffed in the bluff of being…
Teflon tuff, scared of the bear of truth, has them
diving under the bed while dreading knowing
what they know…

They live in strife, unaware they are a scared-
'T' cat on the inside, hiding inside their pride,
disallowing listening…

Blistering the cosmos with burping BS showed
me the door of the insane of the same, unlocked
a new me to discern to learn in order to earn a
cascading cash flow...

With a respondent mind I am divinely fine being
a proponent moment and opening new avenues
of parvenu peace, applauding real virtuous
energy, nurtures unlimited prosperity...

From my core curio unbridles my gallant brio to
savor my genuine hero; liberating people...

From their ingrained speculations binds the
mind with their intuitional-'eye'-zed
categorization of stagnation from history...

With an old mindset that anybody or anything
thinks different than society hierarchy is wrong,
insolvent and living wide of the marked way...

That statement is a lily-livered fable people
have been told since the beginning of time.
Keeping the world stabled in fables of 'I know
what is best for you,' has to be let go of right
now...

Highlighting my heart's prominence saying,
"Happy Thanksgiving," to all in a swanky,
thankful, delightful way...

As I boldly say:

Hooray!

Hooray for my parade of peace on earth because of the common sense communiqué of prayer, animating real ardent decree, electrifying...

My holiday spirit in a glorious, godsend way; authorizing me to say...

I aspire for you to relish a Happy Thanksgiving in a picture perfect way...and in Divine Order, NOW!

My Thanksgiving Living is My Heartfelt Giving

My Thanksgiving living is my heartfelt giving opens the way for my heart hallowedness to be my game; to expand my canonized abilities throughout ethereal ethers of the universe…

Enriching my soul and opening my heart to send out unconditional love which allows me to prosper exponentially…discovering new profound endowment within my winning whims of wisdom…

Electrifying my neon discernment, optimizing wisdom, manifesting and ennobling new things from my rich, robust, imaginative charisma - harmonizing my life experiences…

To understand I see wealth in others as a way to play soothsayer 'Santa Claus' - charismatically animating rich élans in a my core décor…

Lighting up peoples' Thanksgiving desires to be experienced in a galvanizing, glorious parade today and every day…in a pristine, pleasurable way…

Opens universal purpose by authorizing people of the cosmos, and me, to prosperously support the rapport by revving-up the universal vista as a highway of astounding, abounding affluence…

With our eyes wide open to see our seas of success by hearing the world opportunities knocking loudly and boldly on our front door, as we open the door to the Promised Land…

As I feel my feet touch pathways of profuse, useful prosperity it unleashes my omnipotent, infinite intelligence by discovering new ways for me to passionately release old ways - sincerely propelling ennobling revelations and initiating telepathic 'YES'-es…

As the way I play in my New Age sagacious world that is the pearl of preeminent enterprising affluence, realizing love unlocks clocks, freeing…

My mind from the linear time and expanding my spiritual serenity to savor the new flavor of lively omnipotence; visualizing everybody as 'wealth-wise' - full of pious pizzazz…

Unsheathing my **razzle dazzle**, revolutionizing avant-garde Zorro zeal by living every moment and discerning ardent zest, zinging lively, hair-raising innovation…

Because I choose to implode the commode of mundane living, the insane of the same, realizing I am the empowered Zorro beaming bold, augur astuteness…

Unleashing my 'Zorro of Tomorrow,' now articulating today's stimulating common sense intentions and igniting intuitive intensity by waving…

My magic wand, fanning preternatural enchantment, unsealing regal, rich, intuitive, natural talent and escalating newborn ingenuity…

Opening the way today for me to play the Yahweh 'YEA'-sayer in my field of dreams, opening the way for my high pay…

Prayer; animating 'YES'-es in all phases of my life equals laser intuition, freeing everything I desire in a fired-up way…

By strumming my steel guitar geniusness and unleashing my gallivanting avatar guitarist who sings my 'I won' songs because I choose to have fun in getting done with waning in the mundane…

Opens the way for me to snow ski on my Swiss Alps of success, feeling my snowboarding of wealth bequeathed to me from a Yule Tide ride…

Televising my Thanksgiving sleigh-ride over

fresh, virgin snow which sparkles with my
lavish avalanches of opulent opulence in a rich,
rainbow way…and in Divine Order, NOW!

Robert A. Wilson

Black Friday Fun

On Black Friday shoppers rise early to be the
bargain-hunting pearls swirling in out of malls,
unfurling their being in a hurry squirrelly way to
arrive and thrive at the mall, early enough to
have a ball. So, I say...

*Happy shopping to one and all! May your day
at the mall be a ball as you stand tall, facing
the brazen craze of the crazy shoppers, gazers,
and grazers.*

They have their blazing laser-beam eyes
gleaming that 'beware of me' stare as they
blatantly seek the fashionable toys for girls and
boys on their list...

As they race across the mall, beware of their
'balls to the wall' head of steam, with rock-n-
roll romp-em stomp-em satire to fire at anybody
who gets in their way...

Ready to use and abuse their body as a bowling
ball so when they are in the 'fink of their over
think'...

Thinking you have YOUR eyes on THEIR
Christmas prize, they hurl their bowling ball
body, seeing you as thin as a bowling pin,
wanting their one of kind present...

Open your eyes to see they encompass a kick-ass take name flame showcasing a thrilling willingness to knock you out of your socks!...

Unleashes your wherewithal to understand 'to stay well' you get the hell out of the way of the 'hoot and hollering' bowling ball squalls...

WOW! Now you are standing tall on stage broadcasting the fact that you are a sage because you stayed out of the fray of the raging craze of shoppers...which has landed you in the mall's 'Hall of Fame'...

Opens way for you to enjoy you holiday spree, decreeing your shopping-wise and praising your 'get out of the way' moxie shows you are a soothsayer 'seer,' relishing your Black Friday experience with galvanizing gusto...

As you aggrandized a fun in the sun day...

I wish you a regal rich Merry Christmas in a suave, serene, Santa Claus way!

Robert A. Wilson

I Am in the Flow of My Christmas Go!

I am in the flow of my Christmas go! Living inside, galvanizing my New Year gusto, because I choose to trust my true reverence - the un-hampering, soulful trendsetter...

To be my optimum oracle, speaking from the heart to allow my willful gist to be a guest in the universe and under the gallant guise of facilitating my life because...

When I let go of woe, I am in the 'flow of my go,' setting free my noble, global gallivant to fly around and see the world as tourist with clout...

To run about seeing what the world is all about. I see the world unfold; I am told that I am bold to receive the gold medal for honing and honoring my inner lore...

To be the explorer of the earthly wisdom; to free my worldly wit by wonderfully opens revolutionizing my lively laudable 'YES!' Wisely igniting the Yule Tide light to glow with...

Gleaming, lively, omnipotent wisdom by winging my idyllic newborn simplicity and opening magical energies; expanding my mystical magic to experience life...

In a Merry Christmas way!

Today and every day in every way, in a picture perfect way...realizing a New Year Divine Order that extends from now to eternity, in the right way, in a loving way, under grace...in a Divine blessed journey.

My Yule Tide Ride Tithes My 'Santa Claus' Wise

My Yule Tide ride tithes my 'Santa Claus' wise
and tantalizes my Christmas Spirit to ring my
true soothsayer resolve. This is my resolution
solution, emancipating me...

To blissfully bless myself for letting go of being
dressed in stress, distressing over everything
that pings bells of hell in my subliminal mind...

With the pun, 'I have to get it done yesterday,'
hellish hallucinations fester and pester my
selfish shallowness as I realize this is a disguise
of nothing more than my 'big-go' ego...

Taunts and flaunts me into hyper-hysteria,
making me feel important in my stubborn silly
ego and stifling the joy of my holiday
experience, thus transforming my prideful
cynicism...

To be my rude 'Scrooge,' binding the mind with
a tailspin that I *have* to be the one pleasing
everybody by doing *everything* as they sit on
their duff...

Cuffs me into hearing the jeers of, "YOU have
to do this for me!" is the ball-and-chain causing
pain in my posterior stress, creating hollow

hallucinations and giving me pollution of an illusion...

That I am running behind and have more to do than I really have do causes the insane of the insane, creating the madness of the mundane...

So when I choose to let go of you disillusioned collusion of my self-inflicted drama that is dictating my trauma of, "I have to do it now!"...

As the plow of disallow stops now and expands my enterprising energies into the fact that **I choose this** now sanctions me to understand...

It is my choice to voice my daily undertakings, taking my egotistical naughtiness out of the equation, faking out my 'I have to do it now!' egotistical haughtiness...

Un-tethers my copious utopia, delighting my heart, letting loose Christmas cheer and revealing a crystal clear paradigm presenting a pioneering Christmas Pizzazz to realize...

I now choose to peruse-N'-cruise - enticing my spicy Christmas Charisma to be the 'POW of my WOW' of prowess. Audaciously and vivaciously setting free Christmas, my spree...

Celebrates my Christmas Extravaganza by liberating my Divine librettist chi and prophesizing my revered, effervescent epiphanies to say…

I play today in a youthful reindeer way!

Unleashing my Noel Nuances reveals my oracle's light that shines so optimistically bright that it unlocks the blocks from people hearts…

Unfetters their real Christmas Spirit by opening their hearts, thus opening their giving and showing their Yule Tide Tithing Spirit to graciously give to others in a rich, spiritual way!…

This opens peoples' eyes to see that Christmastime is the prime time to receive their Yule Tide Gifts, unsealing their undaunted clout, portraying their real Christmas Charisma!…

So now I bless my Christmas Spirit, which also blesses me. I am authorizing my canonized adeptness to decree my Christmas Spree is free in the universe!...

To boldly say: "Merry Christmas to one and all!" May your Holiday Season in this holly-jolly time of year ascend to greatness, as I see your sphere of spiritual abundance beam with gleaming…

Genuine love, emblazing the amazing New Year glory which enlivens my Christmas Cheer in a keen, 'Rudolph the Red Nose Reindeer' way!

My Prosperity Eyes See the World as an Enterprising Sleigh Ride

My prosperity eyes see the world as an enterprising sleigh ride to chime and rhyme in my subliminal mind; to understand I expand when I listen; I glisten with lithe canonized abilities...

To glide and slide into my mammoth 'money making universal opportunities' with my listening eyes wide open and my ears hearing my own 'saintly' patience, I understand that I expand my wisdom...

I amplify my adept people skills, poise and facilitate my daily encounters with spirited, magnetized communication which unlocks the blocks...

On my cascading cash flow and streams of cash-paying clientele that swell my wealth to propel me into being a world traveler...

Because now I understand I have opened my prosperity eyes, seeing the world as an adventurous endeavor forever to fly...

Like Santa - through the night - unleashing my entrepreneurial wise to feel the realness, televising that I am the Nobel Prize winner to the world. My groundbreaking innovation...

My risk-taking stallion galloping across the galaxy at breakneck speed with my omnipotent eyes open and ready with my laser-guided sixth sense sensing *every* new salient energy in...

The universal ethers as I expand my tenacious hegemony, energizing a real 'state of the art' acuity catapulting my intuitive agility into free-flowing inventive reality...

Shaking my inner scenery with an earthquake awakening that coined the limericks in my sublime phonons, enlivening my proton neutrons into nu-CLEAR visions...

To experience rapturous copiousness by relishing my parvenu paradigm and signing on the bottom line - royally dining on a 'cloud nine' of astuteness I audaciously, vivaciously toot...

My horn; dauntlessly shows my astute new attitude. I am a daredevil child on the loose with a Pink Panther prowess, cutting loose my Dr. Seuss 'hull-a-bal-loo,' let's do a society, taboo...

Take action on a innovative idea; brilliantly open omniscient visions to experience life in dashing desire by lighting the fire under my lavish luxury, spinning the world...

Like a top, electrifying an expansive whirlwind of a copious utopia to roust out the prodigious potentate in the universe with a vim and vigorous swagger, telepathically giving my potentate prowess...

A swift kick in the posterior to arouse my savant savvy - to sagaciously broadcast my sassy, preeminent prophecies by brashly telling the world filled with adversity of perversity...

That I am a soothsayer - a warrior seeing adversity and perversity as raw, unrefined wisdom with a heart full of 'unconquerable valor.' This unclenches my iron-will, setting free...

My trailblazing titan that seeks to then stoutheartedly see the light of wisdom in the adversity and perversity, listening for my peerless 'winds of wisdom' to blow...

My breezes of bountiful brilliance into my subliminal landscape. This plants my seeds of philosophizing sapience in conscious awareness, expanding adversity into amplified ability...

Energizing perversity into enterprising prosperity opens out my gallant, valiant visions of plush universal...

Affluence, which frees my innovative 'wise' and opens my inventive eyes allowing me to hop the opportunity - understanding *op-port-unity*...

As I 'hop the op,' sailing to the port of unity in the cosmos community, unleashing my preserving seer to steer my stalwart stallion right through the hell-of-a egotistical blue 'ha-ha'...

I now understand challenges are thrown in my face and blown out of proportion by my naughty haughtiness which allows me to be a mountain mustang, scaring...

The fright right out of the ingrained pain of the 'robber baron' which hides in my subconscious mind like Saddam Hussein in a cave, expressing raving lunacy...

But lacking a backbone and damn empty on bold bravery, reveals a razor-sharp newness in my subliminal sapience because I now realize...

The ego rides a phony pony of scared-'T' cat-'I'-tice - relying on the lies of fear, pinning its inner *depend-a-site-ice* that binds the mind to be addicted to criticize and whine...

About everything that has went awry - crying to everybody then criticizing everything that everybody does to energize the entrepreneurial ideas. Because I now recognize my egotism of ism, I sell myself to my internal controlling cynicism that is the lousy louse placing the polarizing doubt in my intuitive landscape. This invokes...

The clouds of doubt in my physical world because I now understand the 'big-go' ego clucks like a chicken licking the wounds of yesterday, smearing fear and doubt. But...now...I have the clout!...

I now realize the ego is a drunken addict in a funk of fear with a sulking, stalking, bully attitude speaking with a dingbat wit...

Expressing the fact that: "I am a selfish weakling full of silly bully BS stuck in the 'stink of my think,' wallowing in my self-centered over think...

Sputtering the uttering, I lack the backbone to stand up for who I am! And the fact that it is now going, going, gone - like a Babe Ruth home run. So, now that the mindset is out of my subliminal park and done...

Opens the way for my 'YEA!'-sayer Yahweh to feel and express this zinging zeal that beams divine white light from my heart, delighting my spiritual sage to say:

I love you all! Merry Christmas to one and all!

Holiday Wisdom

*May your Christmas be blessed with zest as
you experience a feisty festive ball in a rich,
regal way...relishing your fun in the sun!*

My Yule Tide Pride Opens My Christmas Eyes!

My Yule Tide pride opens my Christmas eyes to
see my holly-jolly Christmas 'by golly!' I love
my Christmas spirit…it sets free my heart's
Holiday delight!…

Lighting up my natural 'Noel' essence
authorizes my pure 'seer' to stay on. The
'dancer' sanctions me to dance, enhancing
Prancer's 'flash dance,' and unleashing
Dasher's dazzling colorful Comet…

Charismatically highlighting Vixen's sunlit wit,
donning Donner's flaunting flair and
unsheathing Cupid's daring heart to stay on as
Blitzen lets me listen to the sprightly Holiday
Cheer!…

Bountifully booming through the universal
sphere, singing "Let's adhere to all people's
embellishing gifts!" The gifts we preeminently
present to each other as we gallantly gallivant
throughout the galaxy…

Gracefully galvanizes the universal vista with a
zealous zest, expressing rambunctious rabble-
rousing 'shaking in the boots'…

Hoot and holler triumphantly while tooting a
rapturous robust, "Reindeer Cheer Merry
Christmas" to one and all. Let's enjoy our Santa

Claus pause to express a heartfelt thanks for this!...

Christmas Extravaganza laudably allows me to blissfully bless everyone in the personal way they ceremoniously celebrate this joyous season, as everyone blesses me...

As I relish my Christmas spree of 'I am free in my heart, soul, spirit, DNA and body, to be in the 'flow of the glow' of this Jovial Jubilee. I share in my heart with one and all!"...

As I blissfully bless my 'Ho-Ho-Ho,' let's get up and go, as we relish a holiday feast forever...

And this day, peace on earth can occur by opening my listening eyes to hear the Christmas Cheer from my inner Christ-Mass...

Sanctions me to amass the brassiness of my awesome spiritual sassiness to shine my inner-Christ's Divine light as my Christ's light takes flight, televising my real rainbow Christmas Charisma...

Unlocks my Yahweh and opens the way for 'YES!'-ing the blessings of my 'YEA!'-sayer's get up and go which allows me to glow in genuine, lively oracle wit...

Enlightens peoples' lives to thrive in exalting their prime time phenomenon because I regal-

eyes the wise in recognizing the winning ways
of Rudolph's bright red nose shinning so
bright...

Canonizes my hallowed realizations and ignites
my luminary lithe, glowing from my core décor
and showcasing my Bethlehem Star by
tantalizing my megastar perkiness, audaciously
applauding...

My appreciation for my 'Kris Kringle' debonair
- dauntlessly expressing bold, optimizing,
newborn, ardent inspirational revelations...

As I say:

***Hooray! Let's play with my child by
unleashing my 'inner' child's Christmas
innocence which instigates a Yule Tide
marriage in my carriage, broadcasting my
mature magic!***

As my internal soothsayer optimist unleashes
my terrific toddler to play this day - and every
day - showing my mature savvy savant that it's
okay to play the game of life just like a kid...to
win!...

So let's begin to show the world I won my game
of life because I chose to be a kid at heart with
the wisdom of a mature monarch in my daily
life...

Sanctions me to say "Merry Christmas" in a charming, childlike wit that exalts from my mature, self-assured heart that darts, daring astute and revolutionizing talent to be the valiant valet…

In my gallant, grown-up way as I open my Christmas Eyes to see the universal spree that celebrates the birth of Christ with the whole family opening their gifts under the tree. In reality the gift…

Everybody sees is you as you open your eyes to see your real gift is your genuine genius innovation freeing your tantalizing talent to unlock that songbook invention within your inventive genes…

Energizes peoples' eyes to see that you are the innovative intuitive, unbinding their mind from the definition of insanity by doing what they have always done and expecting different results catapults…

You into the new frontier as the adventurous 'seer.' Seeing your pure, clear sunrise is what highlights your inner prize…

And unleashes a new panoramic vision of vim and vigor, igniting superstar intuition and opening your Christmas Eyes to see the gift you really are to the universal supply of canonized wise…

New frontiers in you intuitive landscape evict the bland counter band in your subliminal mind because you have expanded into the prudent parvenu of: "I can do anything now!"…

Because I am in the "WOW of NOW with POW," pronouncing profound prophesying oracle wizardry which articulates the perpetual motion of my broad rainbow brilliance…

Because I encompass the resilience to be brilliant in silence by singing *Silent Night*; my soul shines so bright that it sends out unconditional love…

Lyricizing a lively liberating "Hark, the Herald Angels Sing," Rob!

I love you all…as we all have a ball experiencing the best Christmas of all!

As I ride my 'Santa Sleigh' saying: "Hey, look at me lounging on my beautiful bountiful beaches of lavish luxury while relishing my Santa Shangri La in the spa of sumptuous prosperity!"…

Blessed as I tour the world in my 'Santa Sleigh,' may your day be as bountifully blessed. As you are a brilliant blessing to me and the world in a Merry Christmas and Happy New Year Way!

And in Divine order…NOW!

I Authorize My Christmas Wise to Allow My Tao to WOW the World!

I authorize my Christmas Wise to allow my Tao to WOW the world with wonderful wisdom in a wonderful way, as I play today in my radiant rays of my real, animated "Yahweh"…

Saying…"Hey! I do play for pay because I can expand my pay when I authorize my inner prize to realize that pay energizes prosperity every day, appreciating 'YES'-ing my ennobling realism…

In my inner self-assured maestro; in the throw of being all 'pro in the go' unleashes my WOW of my Tao into the view of people in this world…

In a swirling, whirling wind I am enamored by the limerick in a rock-n-roll free-fall, stating that I encompass it all so I win innovatively by naturalizing dauntless determination within to express success to…

Others. Because I choose to win by opening the way for me to confess success, I see others as they sashay through their daily endeavors, forever enterprising their winning ways within their skin…

As I relish an entrée of omnipotent peace,
astonishing 'YEA'-sayer soothsayer smoothness
by rousting out an astounding realism that links
my unusual sassiness, expanding life with lithe
idioms…

I decree that I open many money streams;
sanguinely tantalizing reverence and enamoring
ardor breathes miracles and unfetter bellwether
that I got it together sets free my fore-fronting…

I fly everywhere avatar, aviator, 'seer' -
unhitching my bitching about anything -
unwound my abounding undaunted utopia…

Unhinging my hell-raisin' bronc-ridin' bro,
showing I won the 'All Round Buckle,'
astounding the world…

As I flaunt my astonishing amour-propre (self-
respect) to applaud significant
accomplishment…

Because I undo the 'hooey' duping of defeat
because I obliterate the 'de' of defeat and
unsheathes my forthright feat to unseat defeat,
unwinding daring expansiveness to cognize
defeat as…

Dauntless emotions, fearlessly expanding
audacious titan triumph to be the omnipotent

'oomph' to realize: "I pet universal wealth and success like a puppy," in plush, prosperous ways...

To unlock my plush prosperity 'YAH'-zing my rococo appeal to be my 'zeal of success' in my internal fame as I see my bold - I told the world - ...

I am a preeminent prodigy, unleashing my vehement visionary to be a 'savvy superstar life force' in the cosmos because I am a titan Taoist with maharishi mysticism that says: "I speak miracles"...

To make all pessimism extinct like a dinosaur opens the way for my rabble-rousing soothsayer to soar, shining my Divine light on the pessimism of the world...

To make the 'fake and bake' of corporate fascism and egotistical fear go awry to cry in the dimness of try - allowing that I sold my soul to corporate droning are now the tears of fear...

Waters my soul, sending out unconditional love lauds me into planting new intuitive paradigms of affluent acuity in my subliminal garden to see my pristine paradise of blossoming riches...

That opens out a razor-sharp wit that fears are my fighters, energizing audacious revelations to be my snappy, dapper, daringness to engage my fears as my friends expand astute reverence...

In my inner landscape to revolutionize my
consciousness - to see fears as unrefined
wisdom - opening out wealth in a stealthy, yet
healthy way, I play this day in a plush,
prosperous way...

I ride the highness of my debonair doctrinaire to
be the 'fresh air' people breathe. I heave out the
smoldering, egotistical 'ick of the thick' as I lick
society's boots expanding out of social
snootiness...

Of the, 'I think they give a hoot about me'
hindsight, hindering my synergy of mystery
unfetters my 'let-er-rip!'...freeing my rococo
'get up and go' to walk in the mystery of
wisdom and see the light of wisdom...

In my situations. I hear the breezes of brilliance
in every circumstance to dance while I plant my
seeds of wisdom in my inner garden...

As I cultivate my wisdom by watching my seeds
of wisdom grow into giant sequoias of sapience
to engage the world with universal clarity by
seeing a nu-CLEAR vision with a *v-v-v-v-
vrooming* veracity...

To engage my clairvoyant cleverness to
understand that I create drama and trauma while
I electrify my karma and dharma to energize my

brio to my hero, to visualize my intentions…

Within my inner landscape. By illuminating my vehement tent I call my spiritual 'let's entertain the internal' realness of who I am, which instantly glows…

With my genius, love, and omniscience wisdom, serving the world with a rare daring heart acumen…today and every day, as I morally say:

I accept, receive and appreciate ME just the way I am!

To love the cosmos with the most magical, oracle sapience tantalizes my appreciation for the universal miracles as I marvel in mystery…

That instantly reveals my sumptuous never-ending flow of my lavish avalanches of Christmas abundances in a Happy New Year optimistic way!

And in Merry Christmas Divine order…NOW!

Merry Christmas

"Merry Christmas one and all! I love you all!"

You are the greatest gift of all to me and the universe as you glow in your Yule Tide aura. As you soar...

Exuding your daring ardor, I love who I am - my innermost host with a singing essence and knowledge that it is a wonderful time to be alive. Rhyming in rococo lets us go to the heaven *hull-a-bal-loo*!...

Doing the piquant perky 'Santa Claus Twist' sends my silvery effervescent glow streaming the gleam of generous love, expansively accenting magnanimous synergy. This opens Holly Jolly...

Holiday Cheer by drinking a bottle of bountiful bubbly, brilliantly beaming Santa Claus sprightliness and opening the right mystical visions to see my magical spree...

Sailing so freely like 'Santa's Sleigh' illuminates my heart's delight, real-'eyes'-ing my Christmas Chi skis the galaxy - aggrandizing my appreciation for the awesome Shangri La R & R. This lets me play...

On Broadway - *Rob Runs Free* unleashes my

Robert A. Wilson

Yule Tide pride to ride the tide of tithing my
core decree which unsheathes my Christmas
karma...

Glistening, charismatic, extraordinary, ecstatic
personality setting free my Tao dharma,
dauntless singing charming Christmas Carols,
lyricizing my enlivened love in the ethers of the
universal vista...

Enhancing my dancing charismatic Christmas
Carols, heralding the New Year by recognizing I
am a precious prize with the cosmos unlocking
my New Year 'seer'...

Because I sent the universe my present,
broadcasting my fluorescently free-flowing,
electrifying, oracle-'eyes'-ing, prodigious
prodigies - bodaciously being a 'WOW'-ed
wizard...

In the universal prowess, gallantly zings my
Santa Claus zeal as I relish and embellish my
family festival by telling the world how swell...

I enjoyed my holiday ball with one and all,
allowing the universal people to feel the real
zest of my soul...sending out unconditional
love...

To see I am the genuine gift I give to the
cosmos shows my rousing bigheartedness and
televises my dauntless ability that you

prestigiously present to the cosmo connoisseurs.
I shine like sun reflecting off the Grand Teton
covered in fresh snow, throwing a bolder-dash
'bash' for the birth of Christ our Savior as MY
Christ within, is my bold intuitive innovator
soaring...

Like the Star of Bethlehem, it mirrors my
soothsayer 'seer' of savvy superstardom. It is
my avatar-star that I ride like a bull rider
winning the Gold Buckle in the National Finals
who sees me walking down...

My yellow brick road paved in brilliant gold
bars as the universe shows me copious dough
allowing me to 'let go with the flow,'
relishing...

The fact that I am prosperity plush, embossing
my impressive path of lavish luxury in a suave,
sure-fire way...and in a Merry Christmas Divine
order...NOW!

I Unleash my New Year 'Seer' By Expressing Rococo Cheer!

I unleash my New Year 'seer' by expressing rococo cheer which elaborates my spry, lively lore that I am for sure ceremoniously celebrating the colossal collaboration of the cosmos camaraderie of…

My physical me and my spiritual spree ringing the bells of twelve - vehemently vibrating my rainbow bliss, I experienced in 'benevolent eleven.' So as I lovingly let go of eleven rings…

'My rococo robust wealth in twelve' effusively epitomizes the synchronizing of my enterprising, astronomical tsunami of my innate innovation. This vitalizes…

My mammoth money stream which flows to me in an extreme prime time fashion as I walk the universal isle in rich robust style, profiling…

My New Year 'seer' as I adhere to my savant soothsayer, shifting into high gear with **New** Year hearing…un-defend what I know…un-shield my feelings to hear everything…

That expands my wisdom by freeing me of my egotistical stigmatisms that imprinted otiose pain, changing me into the Prima Dona of drama, transforming drama into internal terrorizing trauma...

In my conscious landscape is now gone like Osama Bin Laden, opening out my feisty frontiersman 'rococo revolutionary wit,' galvanizing my genuine energizing astute resolute...

Tooting my potentate horn and hallowing my omnipotent *real* New Year's resolution:

I am the New Year Seer!
I wear the Talisman of Tao in 2013!

Avowing the 'WOW' of my audacious visions optimizes my sumptuous wealth, igniting my newborn genius and unbridling by moneyed-up wise by opening my money eyes to **see** money...

As a synergizing energy from my inventive genius highlights my bright newborn passion to be sassy, correlating daily events with my enterprising 'eyes' wide open all the time...

Seeing my local living area, entrepreneurial playground, emphasizes my bold, golden, global, trendsetter titan that exudes gallant 'get up and go,' galvanizing the galaxy brio...

With my innovative hero's modernized

ingenuity, because my daily encounters enriched my charismatic character and enhanced my rococo resolve as well as expanded prestigious patience...

Actuating my forthright foresight by engaging my lightning bolt enlightenment by mesmerizing the universal vista with my manifesting magnetism which unlocks this new paradigm...

In my 'wisdom of magnetism' is 'my omnipotent-ism of magnetism' - I serve mankind in a wonderful wizard way that portrays my array of talents. Balancing...

My wisdom announces my profound 'MY' wins because I am the wise inventor, naturalizing my adept abilities to understand that I think my way to stress and I facilitate my way...

To success unleashes this parvenu prodigy. I now do what I did as a kid, so now I am a kid at heart, darting my smart sharp wit with an unconquerable attitude. I surrender to my dreams, realizing...

My dreams are my real dauntless robustness, electrifying and animating magnificent dreams by correlating perky vibrations with a majestic matrimonial saturation for the duration, spurring...

My assured doctrinaires and showcasing my superstar talent on the red carpet because I married my dreams' intuitive wit and innovative inspirations with the wisdom gained from my daily encounters...

Suavely sauntering on the carpet ride, ringing the bells of twelve and singing 'Glory' to my lively life story, I now relish my never-ending stream of beaming copious copiousness...

As I am drinking ceremonious sherry, I prosperously see the world swirl in a swishing sassy affluence. Showcasing my debonair flair, I say: "Happy New Year!" to you in a magical cool way.

Today and every day I ring the 'bells in twelve' thanks to the mystical, magical and physical sources in the universe that have extended the extravagant wealth in twelve...in a genuinely great way, and in Divine order...NOW!

Happy Easter

When you choose to peruse this particular *Cowboy Wisdom Innovation Coaching Vibrant Vision* you choose to open your inner prowess.

You allow yourself to eavesdrop on new worldly wisdom, visualize your desired life, taste 'moneyed-up' milk chocolate success, smell the roses, listen to your inner acumen and feel the words energize your inquisitive entrepreneur.

You authorize your wealthy inner success to explode as you relish the experience these visionary words offer by expanding your inner landscape.

———

You broaden Easter to one and all. May your day be as blessed as you are a blessing to me and the world, showcasing your pious pearls of peace and emotional affluence, revealing love by...

Saying to the world: "I chime new prime time rhymes in the universal vista, broadcasting a bold, shiny spiritual spree" to tell the world that I am free and I am *here* to free!...

The world from mundane monotony unties my
flying flare to dream the extreme and
audaciously dare my rare, emotional,
enterprising energies to synchronize, synergize
and jazzercise…

My heart hegemony, endorsing the 'buzz' - the
bold, utopian, zealous zeal unlocking the pep in
people's steps by allowing the awesome
deftness to expose…

The entrepreneurial wise…unrestricting people
to allow them to open prosperity eyes to see
their opulent opportunities flow to them this
Easter Day. As Jesus was resurrected today, I
revolutionize…

My wholehearted will to expand the world in
wisdom; energize omnific, terrific, intuitive
innovation in the heart wise, un-cluttering the
universal highways and bi-ways…

Of Divine love to flow. Thereby unleashing
worldwide omnipotent, poetic peace NOW in a
cooperating, cascading, abundant way because I
love to play this Easter Day engaging…

My innermost godly supremacy to win my game
of life when I UN-defended my genuine,
amazing magnetism by electrifying my Divine,
drinking my Screaming Eagle wine…

As I sashay, enjoying my profuse, prominent

wealth, health and wisdom in my kingdom of
mystical, magical realm of miracles, energizes
my heavenly harmony...

Un-tethering my white-feathered revered
ascendancy unbridles my collaborating
competency, entrancing new-fangled dauntless,
deific, terrific willing, internal jive with
inspired...
Alive wittiness to realize the Easter Bunny plays
in a witty imaginative way today. Allowing
people to enjoy the prophetic foresight of this
Easter Extravaganza opens a family Bonanza...

In a bona-fide, boundless, brilliant way as my
imagination engages my inner sage - paging my
savant sage to philosophize my prophet prowess
- unsheathing...

My wonderful worldly WOW!-ess, mirroring
walking out of Medieval Ages and landing in
the middle Disney Land, experiencing rainbow
bliss with every breath I experience, to instantly
witnessing...

The embellishment of Easter with a loving
heart, a peaceful inner landscape, and physical
splendor that mirrors the mountain beauty and
ocean opulence that the world displays...

To soothing our eyes; to pleasuring our noses -
this enlivens our listening and harmonizes our
hearing, tantalizing our taste buds to bountifully

bloom in the magnanimous, bold, never-ending flow...

Of abundance this Easter in a Divine, blessed way...in a heart loving way - in the RIGHT way under grace, in a idyllic serenity and in splendid Divine order...NOW!

Boost a Toast

I boost a toast to you with a smile on Cinco de Mayo, just as *I'll Have Another* won the Kentucky Derby, mirroring me, telling the cooperating cosmos…

I am a twin of *I'll Have Another*. I am a winner! I am experiencing superb success as I judiciously understand that I have won my life Kentucky Derby-style…

As I dauntlessly dare myself to vehemently vision ME - witness ME - living in my copious copiousness today and every day in every way, realizing…

I express and experience brilliant bold 'YES'-es, beaming from my heart an eminence that reveals my peerless preeminent stallion to race with brash craziness…

To understand brash craziness canonizes rebellious autonomy, zealously invigorating neonatal, entrepreneurial, superstar savvy by parading my valiant valor and fluently fortifying…

My spirited warrior guts-iness sanctions my daily encounters to move along in a silky smooth groove like the gallantly gallivanting *I'll Have Another*…

As I blazingly run amazingly smooth, honoring
my conquering titan soul as I fluidly fly across
the finish line at Churchill Downs, realizing my
run for the roses...

Ended in lavish luxury - boosting a toast to my
Cinco de Mayo by saying 'My-O'-My - I
express profound percipience which showcases
my stouthearted stallion stamina, telecasting...

My cheeky classiness, striding like a mountain
bred mustang running full speed across the
Shoshone Mountain thoroughfares...

Stopping to inhale the splendor of the Wyoming
Wilderness subliminal mind, to confess that I
am on my own. I am alone on a Lewis and Clark
expedition, seeing the beginning of Atlantic
Creek and Pacific Creek...

I begin on the Continental Divide in the Teton
Mountains as I calmly experience the quietude
of mountain scenery where motorized
machinery is disallowed...

My eyes are ardently allowed to be avowed by
nature's pristine panoramic preciousness,
mirroring my visions of my inward serenity as I
watch the Elk racing through the trees,
showcasing their spiritual spree...

As the Elk run so gallantly free through the trees

where man is unable to walk, this mirrors the
fears of people in their physical waddle - dilly
dallying in their 'pity me' puddles of mundane
dawdle…

Fuming blame, inflaming society's structure is
instantly imploded like Fort Steuben Bridge,
letting go of my rickety bridge between my
trying to fit into society and thinking I know
everything…

Endorsed my enthusiasm into being a flexible,
forthright listener to my Wapiti (Elk) Wisdom.
This unleashes my Jim Bridger wilderness
intuitive intuition…

Mirrors the Elk running through the trees of Jim
Bridger's National Forest landscape authorizes
my sovereign serenity to soar in order to survey
my innovative landscape…

Photocopy's an eagle circling the Grand Teton,
showcasing eagle majestic magnificence to the
eyes of people who are in awe of the eagle's
panoramic grandness brands…

My sand to expand through and beyond the
nauseating nuisances of the societies' ordinary -
showcasing how I won my wealth game like *I'll
Have Another* won the Kentucky Derby…

Highlights my thriving life-force portrait -
pictures of my winning divinity standing in the

universal 'winner's circle' at my very own
Kentucky Derby to be prestigiously proud
speaking out loud...

With my wreath of roses wrapped around my
neck because I chose to run at breakneck speed
and televise my heart of a champion to the
world as I stand tall because I gave it my all...

In the 'winner's circle,' aggrandizing my
listening lithe to understand **I won** as I boost a
toast to you with a smile and wish you a Grand
Time on Cinco de Mayo!...

As I smile, my will to power my credence
embellishes my gallant stallion within me,
sanctioning me to smell my roses of rich
opulence. Seeing every sunrise...

I sign my sun-up pre-nup within me to be a
better person today and every day, in every way.
As I unsheathe my pre-dawn daringness...

I spawn plush, prosperous outcomes - exalting
in my exhilarating dawn which unravels my
rabble-rousing resolve to dream audaciously...

Walking revitalizes my willpower, animating
my lively Kentucky Derby imagination,
naturalizing genius within my inventive
wilderness, igniting newborn invention which
unravels...

My new, endless, cascading cash flow to sit comfortably contented on the front porch of my Grand Teton Villa, rocking in my chair and enjoying keen tranquility relishes…

My Teton Mountain sunset in a pristine, rich, bountiful way…under grace in a heart-blessed loving way. And in Rocky Mountain Splendor Divine order…NOW!

Honoring Memorial Day

'Eye' so appreciate the men and women who serve our country in the Armed Forces today - and in yesteryear. They have allowed me to enjoy the freedoms I experience. This Memorial Day - and every day - I send prayers of genuine gratitude and heartfelt love to the families of the women and men serving in the faraway lands, in this country, as well as to the children, spouses and families that have lost loved ones who gave up their own lives to ensure the citizens of the United States that they would have their freedom. They, above anyone else, have galvanized our way of life.

I thank the gallant men and women in the military who sacrificed their blood and life in foreign lands and in our native land, emancipating the world from the egotistical dictators, such as Osama 'dimwitted' Bin Laden, Al-ca-ca and all their leaders, the vengeance of Hitler, the insane Hussein - they all deserved to die without the taking of the lives of our men and women.

This Memorial Day we honor those who stormed the beaches of Normandy, walked the Ho Chi Min trail, the evil streets of Baghdad, battlefields of Iraq, Afghanistan, the trails of Torah Bora. We honor the S.E.A.L. team that invaded the compound of Bin Laden - the warriors lost on both sides of the Civil War battlefields, Flanders Field, Pearl Harbor, Battle of the Bulge, Pakistan - and all the other confrontations that allowed the people of the world to understand they have an alley against oppression. And, here, in the United States, we miss and love those men and women who paid the ultimate price for us to live the constitutional rights we are entitled to.

The men and women who sacrificed their lives deserve the ultimate respect, love and heartfelt gratitude from this world, this country and me - because they walked into the battle with the heart of lion, the willingness of a gunfighter, the gallantry of noble warriors, and they engaged their terra incognita.

Terra is earth…therefore, the gutsy warriors walked the war zone with an omnipotent courage. Understanding incognita is their winning willingness to sashay into the unknown in order to save 'freedom.'

Our military walks into the unknown - today and every day - audaciously accepting the task with the zeal of a trailblazing pioneer. While some come through unscathed, some encounter the sacrifice that has them crossing the river and climbing the mountain to sit on the throne of honor. With a keen understanding they won their game of life by opening the way for the world, this country, and me to have the adventurous opportunity to recognize that freedom flows to those who let go in their unique way.

Freeing the world, the people of the United States, and me to hear the winds of sagacity sprouting seeds of wisdom, expanding the populace and me into a giant sequoia of sapience to see the world as an enterprising playground; to experience life with galvanizing gusto through the triumphant terrific-ness of our military. As they walked (and still walk) into battle - they fought fearlessly, honorably, with a clear understanding that they had the backs of their fellow soldiers.

As people of the United States go to sleep and wake up in the morning, we all encompass a sense of secure freedoms because of our military...which I feel this country's politicians take for granted.

Today, our so-called 'elected' officials pay outside contractors more money than they do our military women and men in the fields of battle. This shows the incompetence of politicians. I have to question the integrity of our leaders - people who will send our sons and daughters to war, yet don't have the guts to pay the people that protect their own families. But today is the day for honor. Memorial Day comes from the heart - nurturing our undaunted resolve and invigorating the natural gallantry by memorial-'eyes'-zing every military solider and showing them - here and above - our ardent love and admiration we have for each and every one of them!

I take a moment today and every day to say 'Aloha' to the men and women in the military, unleashing my chi to send Reiki Energy with a forthright 'Aloha Spirit.' With 'Alo' meaning in the presence of the moment, and 'ha' being my breath sending the essence of life to all the soldiers.

I hope they understand that the love in my heart, valor in my spirit, wisdom in the winds of the world are something I send with my Divine love, energy and light to every soldier who is opening the way for the rest of the world to recognize those ultimate men and women are in the hearts and prayers of all their countrymen today…and every day…in the right way under grace, in a picture perfect way.

Unlatching this new premise: a war is never over until the last wounded soldier crosses the river and climbs the mountain to God, Mrs. Universe - the womb of enterprising energies - the world, this country, and me. In my eyes and heart every servicewoman and man is a Congressional Medal of Honor recipient for their willingness to allow the people of this country to do everything they choose.

As this world heads to picnics, barbeques, the beach, or lounging around in opulence - remember that this has occurred because of our Founding Fathers, people who stood in picket lines, and our military who have stood and are *still* standing for the Eagle - allowing the people of the United States to soar with the Eagles until eternity.

I send regal respect, unconditional love and soulful appreciation to the Queens and Kings that are in, or have been, in the military from the very beginning.

You are gallant. You are unequaled. You are loved. You are missed...
Founding Father Foresight

Infinite Spirit, I give thanks on today - July 4th - from the Great U.S. of A. as we celebrate our Independence. I thank our patriotic founders from the Revolutionary War to today...

I am sending a heart flowing, unconditional, loving 'thank you' to everybody that has, or ever will serve, in the United States Military and all our Allies. Because of our military's courage I am free to write this today and play in a country of free, innovative entrepreneurs.

As I say "Thank You" to the military and all the people of the United States and the world with whom I am experiencing my enterprising journey with today and every day, in the right way under grace, in a proud perfect way, and in Divine order…NOW!…

My forefather foresight ignites my Betsy Ross emancipated classiness to flash a crazy thundering wit, collaborating regal awesome zeal, 'YES'-ing my sovereign journey and freeing my inner spree…

To feel the 'decree of freedom' that flows from within my inner liberated enthusiasm to let go of spasms in my soothsayer eagerness - quickly quit spamming me with quacking quackery…

From my daily life. Instead, I emancipate my founding father foresight to right my ship of success because I sashay through my day with nomad mobility, showcasing my Betsy Ross glossy ability…

To sow new seeds of sagacious, enterprising, emotional discernment - soaring in canonized roaring 'Paul Revere Pride' to ride - opening my autonomous riches, intuitively nurturing…

Galvanized genius to saunter on to my battlefield of negativity which is a humanoid fantasy of false, apathetic, timid, asinine, silliness…

Because I bought into society's mundane 'muck,' so I shucked my mundane 'yuk-it-tee'

muck like an ear of sweet corn as I am now
sworn to my constitutional freedoms within my
skin...

So I shamelessly sent the dreary dreariness to be
instantly consumed in a flame of forthright love,
animating majestic emancipated 'oomph' to
flow through my interior landscape, mirroring...

The Founding Fathers' signing of the Bill of
Rights and enacting the Constitution as MY way
of life; to strive in freedom, arrive in innovation,
thrive in the American Dream...

Life. Liberty. The Pursuit of Happiness. These I
instantly realize and the entrepreneurial wise
opens out an internal consensus when I feel
emotional trepidation rising...

That is telepathically, effusively exciting my
triumphant titan. I am being bitten by a lack of
courage to listen and I am ready to defrost the
frostbitten brought forth by my egotistical
arrogance...

Of 'I am right' instigates blight of slight, living
in the night of nothingness, negating new
wisdom to enter my cognitive communication of
invigorating new nirvana, expanding wisdom...
Because of haughty egotism I create selfish
malice with the need to maintain my level of
mediocrity through mundane, insane conceit -
contritely causing the ego to crave a pat on the

back...

For something that is a natural act of 'exact' as I now realize conceit is control - ostentatiously negating cooperation, omitting living my desired life because I *had* to be right...

I went 'Dah!' Because I suddenly grasped the fact that I shut off my hearing and refused to listen to the peerless percipience in the enterprising exchange...

Because I want to change, as I promptly apprehend the apathetic suspect. I lacked the guts to expand...

So now I understand that change maintains the mundane that has me forever and always - in all ways - circling havoc, admonishing the 'new' and getting evicted from my game of life...

Because change inflicts pain from previous experiences that are re-enacted in this moment, I now real-'eyes' I never ever had a past. I experience a continuous NOW...

Un-cluttering my every day events activates ingrained imprints and opens my frontiersman fortitude to realize I encompass my founding father foresight, emancipating my Betsy Ross classiness...

To sew my flag of financial freedom, I instantly

understand I choose to expand through life by unleashing my prudent power in my neonatal NOW! This unbridles my newborn omnipotent wisdom…

Sets me immediately free from the things that people always say they want and need. I open out this new premonition of intuition when people say 'want' and 'need' - folks foolishly…

Live in the 'daunt of want' and in the weeds of need, creating a disingenuous doppelgänger in peoples' minds - they are peeing in a patch of poverty poison ivy…

Crassly causing a priggish itch to boringly bitch about their life and gossip about what is wrong in other folk's situations because people's expectations…

Enrage doppelgänger deliriousness, smearing their fear and antagonizing their anger caustically causes their pandering to their own slacking curiosity living inside society with a perilous lack of wisdom…

As I instantly realize it is easier to peevishly bitch to itch my egotistical asinine-ness; to transform into less feeling, lousy, egotistical, silly sameness by spamming the world for scams. The time is now…

'BAM!'-med into oblivion as I am instantly

invoking the prodigious-ness of my
Constitutional Rights to take flight in my Divine
light, opens my opportunistic insight…

To the right, innovative endeavors as I promptly
realize the Constitution is suavely simple law;
the easiest way to experience life unveils my
pristine serenity within me to understand…

*Constitutional law unsheathes unity within my
heart to dart daring audacity, revving-up my
tenacity to love another willfully, laudably,
animate wisdom living in affluent wealth…*

*Now to eternity, because the founding fathers
encompassed the foresight, and Betsy Ross
classiness emancipated the country with their
abilities to adapt with a regal sassiness...*

Until the people allowed society to plow their
freedoms - laws of disallow unleashes my feisty
'POW to WOW' the world with a parvenu ado,
adamantly disbands society's damning,
disallow…

As 'We the People' instantly open our new Bill
of Rights Innovation - WOW the blue collar
encircles superstar talent to lead the white collar
out of the ho-hum doldrums…

Because blue collar encompasses bold, lively,
undaunted, enterprising, capitalistic, luminary,
levitating, astuteness - revolution-'eyes'-ing the

world with intuitive innovation...

As 'We the People" realize our enterprising
wise, worldwide entrepreneurial 'get up and go'
appears as I open my eyes to see the world,
exuding prudent wisdom, opulent riches and
luminary determination...

Unleashes an intrepid, inventive sensation,
effulgently enlivens the earthly ethers with
newborn cooperation as the barriers of race,
creed and religion are gone like yesterday's
dawn...

Recognizing the world has been taught 'war'
admonishes depressions like the sun doesn't
shine on a cloudy day as I open my eyes to
understand war...

Unlocks the blocks - the misery of history;
nullifying the lies of war unfetters new acuity
that war is started and artificially inseminated
by whacko's archaically ruining people's
lives...

With whacky aberration, reeking with
bureaucratic BS. History breeds egotistical
archaic leaders such as Hitler, So insane
Hussein and many others...

Because they want their name in the marquee of
history, foolish arrogant leaders feel a need to
inflict their internal misery...

Into the physical world to massage their egos as
I open my heart to appreciate the United States
military...

Yet I question the leadership of my country as
my founding fathers suggested with questions to
expand the country's wealth and Divine
grandeur through innovation...

As my Constitutional Freedoms expand,
energize, and enterprise the experience of my
life inside galvanizing gusto, embellishing the
life, liberty and pursuit of pristine, prosperous
peace...

Obliterating war and the fantasy of war being a
way to change from living in a depression to
living in prosperity, simply because war puts
people to work while the military is protecting
the rest of us...

As I open my sovereign eyes I quickly conclude
omniscient peace flowing from an
entrepreneurial energy expands newborn
revelations, gregariously yahooing...

My Yahweh aggrandizes my heroic-wise,
epitomizing, hallowed hegemony to show the
world my winning, omniscient, regal, liveliness
- declaring the world free from history's
mistakes...

By opening peoples' eyes to see that omnipotent peace is uncontrollable prosperity, energizing affluence, canonizing entrepreneurial effrontery, unraveling self-inflicted despair in the world...

Untying the bald-faced lies of the elite's history, revving up pert copious utopia in peoples' hearts - allowing me to sail on my ship of 'Hallowed Health - Financial - Spiritual - Personal Freedom'...

In an endless, lavish, luxurious way - now until eternity - in the right way, in a loving way under grace, in a pristine perfect way, and in a serene Divine order...NOW!.

Robert A. Wilson

My Mind Is Clear and Visions Are Pure

My mind is clear and visions are pure; my heart is light like the fuse on the Fourth of July Fireworks in Central Park as I glide on to the floor…

To unwind the bind of my undaunted newborn wisdom, opening-out a never-ending ,dazzling discernment by applauding my zooming zeal and 'living in-the-moment' by naturally globetrotting; expressing…

My enterprising wise and waking innovative sapience in every body to free the world - opening the way for sumptuous prosperity to be realized by everything and everybody…

Because folks untree'd their need of greed, buried the taunt of want, unshackled the lack in their poverty conscious to clear their mind - freeing the mind's eye and allowing their visions to be pure…

Undoing their 'woo-woo-ing' and introducing the producing pioneering sprightliness to 'light the bright' in their omniscient essence by unleashing the kapish of…

Their opportunistic landscape, kinetically

galvanizing their intuitive scenery and
unlocking the locks of their innovative
inventions, expanding the universal landscape...

To experience life in a easier, more effortless
way as they unbound their wound-up egotistical
haughtiness to see the sassy, sapient spree
allowing them...

To be them by unwinding their mind to clear;
untying the strings of yesterday's 'show glow'
of their genuine liveliness, optimizing wisdom
to be the gallivanting savant in their daily life...

Opening out their canonized, cascading cash
flow as I play on my beaches of bountiful,
expanding affluence and correlating harmony by
energizing sassy success in every facet of...
My life - living by surfing wave after wave of
wealth - today and every day in a cherished
way, and in Divine order...NOW!

My Cowboy-Up Grit Unleashes My Cowboy Wit!

An audacious Labor Day to one and all!

This is for the men and women who stood in picket lines in order to allow you and I to be free of child labor and sweat shops.

My cowboy-up grit unleashes my cowboy wit; it unwinds my mind to see me birthing my sired desires, relishing my prosperous preferred outcomes from my intrepid intentions...

So now I experience my rich robust results in my daily victorious voyages as I walk down avenues of affluence, embellishing living inside my...

Opulent outcomes. I visualize every majestic mountain-top, blissfully unsheathing my genuine genius to open my listening prowess to hear the highland winds of acumen...

To taste the mountain 'cuisine' of success; to feel the mountain air enlightening the brightening of the sapient spree of my innermost revered resolve, to open out my enterprise wise to ask this question:

How am I, a mountain woman/man on my

***inner trailblazing journey, to relish
experiencing the robust riches I so richly
deserve, and are worthy to realize in all phases
of my spiritual experience?***

I ride the open ranges of my terra incognita
unlocking my forthright visionary. Setting free
my mountain man grit unleashes…

My warrior wit, mirroring the mountain
women/men that paged their galvanizing guts,
untying their winning Cowboy Wisdom to take
audacious 'cowboy-up' action on their plan…

To expand the world by letting loose their
hullabaloo hellion because they touted their
mountain skillfulness un-pasturing their stout-
heartedness…

In their core décor as they undauntedly
understood they were too hard headed to quit
and far too stubborn to turn back, therefore…

They broadcasted their iron-will through
mountain ranges to go where they chose to go
with the patience of a saint, touting their eagle-
eyed scouting abilities to read the physical
landscape as well as ride their innermost open
range of…

Their terra incognita, showcasing their cowboy-
up grit to ride the range of unreal-'eyes'-ed
wisdom that opened the West by unbinding their

pioneering spine, unbridling...

Their inner 'bear' and releasing their brazen, bold enterprising, avatar - realizing their supreme dreams by unlocking their savant sage to free their revolutionary resolve...

To be the tenacious trailblazer; to emblaze their purposeful path by engraving their names of parvenu in the paradise of the West today, as people survey western lands in a tourist, fantasy way...

Opening out people's conquistador curiosity and unleashing real, adventurous genius by electrifying their core curio to ask this quasi question:

How do I open up my mountain woman/man heroic curio to unlock the locks on my cowboy-up grit to unleash my cowboy wit in order to ride the open range of my terra incognita?

So now I choose to mount the mustang to ride the ranges of my terra incognita with mountain man mysticism, recognizing that my warrior wisdom is inside me...

So now I have the grit to go within me to ride my white light mountain range and listen to my silent rivers of wisdom, seeing my seas of sapience flow into my oceans of omniscient omnipotence...

To glow with genuine love, opening the 'WOW!' of my daily experiences, authorizing me to be the triumphant teacher of my journey...

As I enjoy my sunlit success, opening out my sea breezes of idyllic serenity and allowing my Yahweh to be free...

To embellish my overflowing, canonized, copious copiousness...I enjoy today and every day, in a tantalizing 'Labor Day' in a thankful way...and in Divine order, NOW!

Halloween Hologram
Happy Halloween to One and All!

May your 'prosperity basket' always and in *all* ways be overflowing in lavish avalanches of affluent abundances…

'Eye' see my Halloween Hologram unifies my Yahweh and physical image, because the corporal image people see is the illumination of my 'God's' eternal light, harmonizing ardent lissomness love and optimistically 'WOW'-ing enlightenment by divinely hearten-'eyes'-ing omnipotent luminary 'oomph' and grand-'eyes'-ing outstanding, magnanimous wisdom; showing the world my willingness…

To expansively express my regal, rich sapience with a true blue understanding and wisdom I express that opens folks to a healthier way to experience life, and opens the way for razor-sharp new sagacity to enter my phenomenal psyche, effusively energ-'eyes'-ing my ingenious magnanimity; tenaciously televising…

My razor-sharp Halloween Hologram unfastens my harmonic autonomy, lavishly launching 'oomph'-a-size-zing wisdom, harvesting opulent luxuriousness, opening out glorious rapture and augmenting magnificent manifestations by realizing those manifestations unbind a sharp, newborn paradigm that...

My manifestations mirror my majestically moneyed-up adventurer; North-Staring my impeccable, forthright, enterprising 'seer' that tantalizes affluence by tethering infinite, opulent nirvana in the pristine prosperity; encoding of my cell's senses, DNA temple, heart, mind, body, soul and spirit...

Permitting my poverty encryptions to effortlessly slip, slip, and slide away into the fires of the sun; sanctioning my impoverished DNA-ingrained poverty consciousness to fly into nothingness...

In the right way! In a loving way under grace! In a perfectly profound way...

Because I am free to expansively expand my gutsiness to grasp my poverty encryption's which are robustly released - now unlocking brilliant sunrays of newborn, enterprising emancipation; broadening my core scenery to emotionally epitomize the 'I am' experience...prosperity reins, optimizing vibrant epiphanies and revering tremendous Yule Tide sensations in every cell of my temple, heart, mind, soul, and DNA...

Unbridling my 100-billion laser beams of

genuine genius from my Halloween Hologram unleashes my forthright love, abundance, sapience, enthusiasm, robustness - boldly expanding avant-garde mature sagacity into the ethers of the cosmos; unshackling my willingness to…

Listen; to expand my common sense rather than to be right and to know that the other person ffrreeeeees my heart healthiness. By fervently fissuring old paradoxes, I am living a human experience because science told me and somebody else believes…

Resplendently releases old worn out beliefs that everything I have read or been taught is for my highest good, unravels a crystal clear hint that you and I were exposed to a poverty consciousness by a societal system that wanted you and I to be sheep instead of savants, unstitching a novel nuance by…

Expansively expanding, energizing, enhancing, enterprising, experiencing - you and I's - the dazzling desired life with galvanizing gusto unshackles a modern cunning cleverness when I expansively expand my wisdom; I energize my innovation and enhance my focus by unleashing my enterprising entrepreneur to experience my "Life of Riley" in a lavishly, leisurely way gives free rein to…

My YHWY Halloween Hologram of pure white

light - the Divine love, Divine energy, and Divine light to soar through the ethers of the cosmos in the supreme ease as I bask in Halloween wisdom and innovation; lively I live and love while singing on Broadway my songs of Halloween appreciation!

Appreciation of my 'God's' eternal light! In an enlivened, enriched way!

Happy Halloween...and Thank You!!!

ABOUT THE AUTHOR

Robert A. Wilson

I hope you enjoyed, ***Holiday Wisdom***. I am
Robert Wilson, NLP Practitioner,
Hypnotherapist, Past Regression Specialist,
Reiki Master, Radio Show Host, Parts
Integration and Time Line Coach.

Cowboy Wisdom NLI Radio is on Tuesday and
Thursday at 8PM Eastern/5PM Pacific and has
reached out to listeners. *Cowboy Wisdom* in
known to open people's eyes so they see their
talent and engage in their intrepid intentions
instantly.

Cowboy Wisdom Innovation Coaching opens

your enterprising listening to unmask your entrepreneurial wise and unleash your canonized abilities so you see **all** the opulent opportunities to experience your copious outcomes in galvanizing gusto - now to eternity.

Cowboy Wisdom Innovation Coaching shows you how to embark on your own journey to energize your financial, spiritual, personal and emotional sovereignty by galvanizing brand new subliminal blueprints that steer you **out** of the world of confusion and **into** the world of wisdom, in order to unleash your entrepreneurial talents. It electrifies your choices and bonds your day to day encounters with your pioneering genius that allows you to real-'eyes' your highest results. By unifying your everyday life and your desired life, you unlock freshly minted understanding to reveal your boundless financial, personal, spiritual and emotional independence in **all** facets of your life, authorizing you to experience your life's purpose and open the gates to your copious cornucopia!

Robert A. Wilson

www.cowboy-wisdom.com

rob@cowboy-wisdom.com

cwbywsdm@gmail.com

Skype: cwby.wsdm

A SPECIAL THANK YOU TO YOU!

On behalf of everyone at Freedom Of Speech Publishing, thank you for choosing Holiday Wisdom for your reading enjoyment.

As an added bonus and special thank you, for purchasing Holiday Wisdom, you can enjoy discounts and special promotions on other Freedom of Speech Publishing products. Visit www.freedomeofspeech.com/vip to learn more.

We are committed to providing you with the highest level of customer satisfaction possible. If for any reason you have questions or comments, we are delighted to hear from you. Email us at cs@freedomofspeechpublishing.com or visit our website at: http://freedomofspeechpublishing.com/contact-us-2/.

If you enjoyed Holiday Wisdom, visit www.freedomofspeechpublishing.com for a list of similar books or upcoming books.

Again, thank you for your patronage. We look forward to providing you more entertainment in the future.

Robert A. Wilson

Holiday Wisdom
By Robert A. Wilson

For more books like this one, visit Robert A. Wilson's
website at:
http://cowboy-wisdom.com/
http://holidaywisdominnovations.com/Info

Printed in the United States of America
The publisher offers discounts on this book when
ordered in bulk quantities. For more information,
contact Sales Department, Phone 815-290-9605,
Email:
sales@FreedomOfSpeechPublishing.com

Freedom of Speech Publishing, Leawood KS, 66224
www.FreedomOfSpeechPublishing.com
ISBN: 1938634225
ISBN-13: 978-1-938634-22-2